W9-DEL-916

WORLD WAR II
The Full Story

Causes and Outbreak

Published by Brown Bear Books Ltd
4877 N. Circulo Bujia
Tucson, AZ 85718
USA

and

First Floor
9-17 St. Albans Place
London N1 0NX

© 2015 Brown Bear Books Ltd

ISBN: 978-1-78121-229-5

Library of Congress Cataloging-in-Publication
Data available upon request

Managing Editor: Tim Cooke
Designer: Lynne Lennon
Picture Manager: Sophie Mortimer
Editorial Director: Lindsey Lowe
Design Manager: Keith Davis
Children's Publisher: Anne O'Daly
Production Director: Alastair Gourlay

Manufactured in the United States of America

CPSIA compliance information: Batch# AG/5566

CONTENTS

INTRODUCTION

The guns of the Western Front in World War I (1914–1918) fell silent on November 11, 1918. The main victors—Britain, France, and the United States—were determined that the conflict would be "the war to end all wars." The peace treaties that followed the war, however, sowed the seeds for future discontent. Just over 20 years later the world would be at war again.

A Flawed Peace

The U.S. president, Woodrow Wilson, had proposed a peace settlement based on a principle of self-determination, meaning that a people should be able to decide how they were governed. When the Treaty of Versailles redrew the map of Europe, however, many ethnic groups found themselves living in countries in which they were minorities.

Meanwhile, the French in particular were determined to weaken Germany so much that it could never attack France again.

→ A conference in Paris in 1919 decided the terms of the peace treaties that ended World War I.

→ A speaker addresses a crowd in Munich, Germany, during an uprising by Hitler's Nazi Party in 1923.

The peace terms imposed on Germany were harsh. It lost territory to its neighbors and the decision to charge it reparations, or compensation for having started the war, left its economy ruined.

Political Extremism

In the political instability that spread in parts of central and southeastern Europe after the war, extremist politics gained in popularity. Right-wing leaders promised to overthrow the peace treaties and lead their countries to glory through aggressive militarism. In Germany, a young politician began to make a name with his fiercely patriotic speeches. He would rise in popularity and eventually lead the world into war again in 1939. His name was Adolf Hitler.

WORLD WAR I AND ITS LEGACY

The roots of World War II ultimately lay in the peace settlements at the end of World War I (1914–1918). The settlements caused great resentment.

When World War I ended in November 1918, Europe had been devastated. Around 50.5 million military personnel and civilians had been killed or wounded. The economies and political structure of most European nations were in ruins. The empires that had dominated central and eastern Europe had fallen. In their place came new states and great uncertainty. People turned to extremist views and politics.

Political leaders met to draw up peace settlements. The treaties they came up with caused great resentment. Many historians believe the treaties made a significant contribution toward the outbreak of World War II in 1939.

→ British troops pass through a devastated area of France in 1916.

← President Woodrow Wilson (left) waves as he arrives in Paris for the peace conference.

WOODROW WILSON

Woodrow Wilson was elected U.S. president in 1912. After German submarine attacks on U.S. shipping, he led the United States into World War I on April 6, 1917. In January 1918, Wilson issued the Fourteen Points, which were his suggestions for the basis of the peace agreements after the war. U.S. politicians refused to ratify the peace treaty, however. They were tired of war and suspicious of European plans.

The Paris Peace Conference

A series of peace settlements dealing with the defeated powers were negotiated at the Paris Peace Conference of 1919–1920. The most important settlement was the Treaty of Versailles. It only dealt with Germany, but its name is often used to refer to the whole series of settlements. Russia, where a Bolshevik (communist) revolution took place in 1917, refused to take part in the

← Vladimir Ilyich Lenin, who led the Russian Revolution, points the way to a communist future.

ПОД ЗНАМЕНЕМ ЛЕНИНА — ВПЕРЕД К МИРОВОМУ ОКТЯБРЮ!

conference. The "Big Three" allies—French prime minister Georges Clemenceau, British prime minister David Lloyd George, and U.S. president Woodrow Wilson—wanted to restore political stability. They excluded a fourth ally, Italy, which resented being sidelined.

The Terms of the Treaty

Largely at the urging of France, the Allies imposed a tough settlement in Germany. The treaty placed territorial, military, and financial demands on the country and forced it to hand territory to its neighbors in the east, north, and

CIVIL WAR IN RUSSIA

In Russia the Bolshevik (communist) Party seized power during the October Revolution in 1917. Russia stopped fighting in World War I and gave up territory to Germany. In spring 1918 civil war broke out as anti-Bolshevik (White) Russians launched a military campaign against the communists (known as the Reds). Despite help from the Allies, the White forces were slowly overcome.

Allied forces left Russia by fall 1919. The civil war ended in November 1920 with the defeat of the Whites.

west. An area west of the Rhine was to be occupied by Allied troops and the Saarland in southwest Germany was to be administered by the new League of Nations. Germany also lost its overseas empire. In Europe, Germany became 13 percent smaller and lost 10 percent of its population. The German armed forces had their numbers restricted, and tanks, heavy artillery, submarines, and an air force were forbidden. A "war-guilt" clause blamed the entire war on Germany and ordered it to pay compensation, called reparations, to the Allies.

⬇ Czech troops fight in the Ural mountains during the Russian Civil War.

German Reaction

The Allies gave the Germans a stark choice: Sign or face invasion. Germany signed, but the "dictated" peace created deep resentment of the treaty and of the civilian politicians who signed it, and of how the Allies had forced it on them. The war-guilt clause was a particular cause of resentment; the reparations threatened to destroy the German economy.

The Treaty of Versailles was criticized by German nationalists. Army officers claimed that the German army had been "stabbed in the back" by civilian politicians, even though defeat in the war was inevitable by the time the politicians asked for an armistice. A promise to

→ The city of Danzig had formerly been part of Germany and most of its inhabitants were German. Under the peace treaty, it was run by Poland. The Germans greatly resented this.

8210. P.Z. - DANZIG. LANGEN MARKT & RATHA

overturn the terms of the treaty would be a key factor in the rise of one right-wing politician, Adolf Hitler.

The New European Map

The peace settlements redrew the map of Europe. The main causes of the changes were the break-up of the Hapsburg empire of Austria-Hungary and the re-allocation of German and Russian territory. Two new countries were created: Czechoslovakia and Yugoslavia. Poland re-emerged, after ceasing to exist as an independent country in 1795. Romania doubled in size. Austria and Hungary, on the other hand, lost land and became smaller.

↓ French troops in the Rhineland look across the river to the city of Koblenz.

New states appeared in central and eastern Europe, but their borders were sometimes illogical. One-third of the population of Poland were not ethnic Poles, and Czechoslovakia was home to more than three million Germans. Many minorities wanted to be reunited with their "homeland."

Farther east, Bolshevik Russia was a reminder of the danger of revolution. European fears about the spread of communism grew after 1919. Bolshevik leader Vladimir Ilyich Lenin set up the Communist International, or Comintern, to encourage global revolution. In 1922, Lenin announced the creation of the Soviet Union. On his death in 1924, Joseph Stalin became the Soviet leader.

The World Beyond Europe

The peace settlements had also made an impact beyond Europe. The territories of the Ottoman Empire passed to Britain and France under mandates from the League of Nations. Britain gained Palestine, Iraq, and Transjordan (Jordan), while France took Syria. The treaty angered the Arabs, to whom Britain had promised independence. It soured relations between the Arabs and the Allies for decades to come.

WAR GUILT

Article 23 of the Treaty of Versailles placed the whole blame for World War I on Germany. The Allies used this as a reason to demand reparations. They charged the Germans $26 billion and made them surrender their coal-and iron-producing areas such as the Saarland. The huge fine ruined the German economy and caused enormous resentment among many German citizens.

KEY THEMES

THE RISE OF EXTREMISM

After World War I, political extremism spread. The communism of the Soviet Union was matched by the emergence of fascism.

In the chaos of postwar Europe, extremists made bids for power, and violence erupted. Extremism grew on both the political left (socialists and communists) and right (conservatives and fascists). It affected not only defeated countries, such as Germany, but also emerged among victors, such as Italy.

↑ German Spartacists carrying rifles take over a newspaper office in Berlin in January 1919.

Communism in Germany

On January 6, 1919, German communists named the Spartacus League occupied government buildings in Berlin. Although Germany was in the grip of economic depression, hunger, and shortages, the population did not rise in revolution. The Spartacists were soon defeated by groups of extremist right-wing paramilitaries, known as the Freikorps.

Postwar Italy

Italy appeared to have little in common with Germany, having ended the war on the winning side. Italy was not as stable as it seemed, however. The value of its currency, the lira, had fallen, so prices rose and businesses went bust; thousands of military veterans joined the huge numbers of unemployed workers. Many Italians were also resentful of their former Allies. Italian nationalists believed that they had been poorly rewarded for losing 600,000 dead in the war.

In March 1919, Benito Mussolini formed a right-wing party, the fascists. The name came from the Latin word *fasces*, which was the name of the symbol of ancient Roman officials. Mussolini wanted to echo Italy's Roman past. He aimed to crush communism and restore Italian self-respect. That made fascism attractive to

⬇ Former members of the German Navy crew a cannon during the Spartacist uprising in Berlin.

THE SPREAD OF COMMUNISM

After World War I many governments feared the spread of communism and revolution by the workers. In 1919, Soviet leaders founded the Communist International (Comintern) to coordinate communist parties around the world. One result was the "red scare" that swept the United States in 1919 and 1920. Many suspected communists were locked up or deported.

FASCISM

Fascism was first adopted by nationalists in Italy in 1919. It spread in response to the growth of socialism and the failure of liberal governments to achieve political and economic stability.

Fascism had broad ideas. It was characterized by nationalism, militarism, dictatorship, and political repression. It rejected democracy in favor of a strong leader. The citizens owed loyalty to the state.

nationalists and war veterans. The attraction grew when a socialist parliament was elected in 1919. The middle classes were already angry about the failing economy. Mussolini's promise to restore order and Italian greatness seemed to offer a solution to such problems. By 1921, the fascists had 250,000 members and 35 members of parliament. In November they became an official political party, the National Fascist Party (Partito Nazionale Fascista; PNF).

Mussolini Takes Power

In October 1922, with Italy still gripped by political crisis, Mussolini declared that he and his paramilitaries would march on the capital, Rome. Instead, King Victor

Emmanuel asked Mussolini to form a government. The fascist leader became prime minister on October 31. Within two years, he had banned all other political parties. Mussolini had convinced the Italians that he offered the only way to avoid revolution, but at the heart of fascism lay violence.

➤ Female "blackshirts" known as squadristi give the straight-armed fascist salute at a rally in 1922.

→ Benito Mussolini was a socialist journalist before he adopted nationalist views after World War I.

The fascists owed their success to the *squadristi*, the paramilitaries who intimidated political opponents. Much of Italy's establishment also shared the fascists' goals. One reason the king had invited Mussolini to become premier was to stop any threat of a communist revolution that would have destroyed the Italian monarchy.

Rise of Hitler

In 1919 in Germany an assembly met to draw up a new constitution. Berlin was the scene of violence between paramilitary groups, so it met in the city of Weimar. Historians refer to the

government it created as the Weimar Republic. While elections took place, uprisings continued. In April 1920, the National Socialist German Workers' Party (NSDAP, or Nazis) called for the rejection of the Versailles treaty and territorial expansion. The next year Adolf Hitler became the party's new chairman.

Germany was in the grip of an economic crisis. It was suffering high inflation, or price increases. A loaf of bread that cost half a mark (Germany's currency) in

HITLER'S EARLY YEARS

Adolf Hitler wanted to become a painter but instead lived in poverty in Vienna. There he developed a deep anti-Semitism and a dislike of democracy. He served with distinction in World War I but was devastated by the peace settlements. In 1919 he joined the new NSDAP as a spy for the army. Within two years Hitler was the NSDAP's leader.

↑ Hitler, photographed here in about 1925, was careful to come to power by constitutional means.

→ Hitler rides with President Hindenburg after becoming chancellor of Germany in 1933.

December 1918 cost 201 billion marks in November 1923. The hyperinflation wiped out people's savings, and Germans grew bitter at the government's inability to solve the crisis.

The Munich Putsch

Hitler tried to take advantage of this anger. On November 9, 1923, he led an uprising, or putsch, in Munich to take control of the Bavarian government by force. The putsch failed and Hitler was arrested and jailed. However, his trial gave him an ideal platform to give the Nazis publicity. The failure of the putsch convinced Hitler that violence alone

would not bring him to power. He began to concentrate on building electoral support. Meanwhile the government ended hyperinflation by introducing a new currency, and new loans from the United States helped cut the amount of reparations Germany owed.

In fall 1929, however, a crisis of confidence struck the U.S. financial markets. The U.S. raised taxes on imports to protect its industry. Other nations followed, and the new tariffs stifled international trade. The resulting slump led to a global depression. Loans to Germany dried up and companies went bankrupt. By early 1933, a quarter of the labor force was unemployed.

Hitler's Rise

Many Germans looked to extremist parties such as Hitler's NSDAP. Even moderate Germans resented the Treaty of Versailles. Hitler appealed to them with his promise to restore Germany to its former position in the world. At the same time he blamed Germany's

problems on an alliance of Jews, communists, and bankers. These scapegoats were based on stereotypes that already existed in German culture, such as the greed of Jewish bankers. Hitler's arguments, plus a use of propaganda, brought the Nazi Party rapid success. In the 1930 election to the Reichstag (parliament), the NSDAP won 107 seats. It became the second-largest party, behind the moderate Social Democrats (SPD).

In April 1932, Hitler ran against President Paul Hindenburg in the presidential election and won 37 percent of the vote. Chancellor Heinrich Brüning feared the Nazis would seize power. He banned the Nazis' private armies: the Sturmabteilung (SA) and the Schutzstaffel (SS), Hitler's bodyguard. Brüning's move was unpopular with the army. In late May, Hindenburg replaced Brüning with Franz von Papen.

In return for Hitler's support, Papen lifted the ban on the Nazis' private armies. Papen called a national election in July 1932. In the election, Hitler's NSDAP emerged as the largest party, with 37.3 percent of the vote. Hindenburg refused to make Hitler chancellor, however. After another election in

Thousands of Nazis gather at one of the regular party rallies staged in Nuremberg.

KEY EVENTS

THE SPANISH CIVIL WAR

In July 1936, the Spanish army rebelled against the left-wing Republican government. Led by General Francisco Franco, right-wing Nationalists took control of much of Spain. The two sides fought a civil war for three years before the Nationalists triumphed. Hitler and Mussolini helped Franco by providing men and weapons.

November, the Nazis were again the largest party in the Reichstag, but Hindenburg still would not make Hitler chancellor. Instead a new government lasted barely two months.

In early January 1933, Papen proposed a coalition government, with Hitler as chancellor and himself as vice chancellor. He convinced Hindenburg that Hitler could be kept under control. Hindenburg finally agreed to make Hitler chancellor. It was a fatal miscalculation.

Hitler Consolidates

Hitler moved to secure his hold on power. He called an election for March. Taking advantage of a fire started in the Reichstag by a communist arsonist on February 27, 1933, Hitler suspended civil liberties. He also insisted on an Enabling Act to make the chancellor all powerful in order to protect the nation. After the March election again increased the number of NSDAP seats in the Reichstag, the Enabling Act was passed on March 23.

Hitler soon used his new dictatorial powers. He outlawed all parties other than the NSDAP and locked up his political opponents in Sturmabteilung-run concentration camps. Hitler also began to take action against Germany's Jews, beginning in April 1933 with a boycott of Jewish businesses. The Nuremberg Laws of 1935 stripped Jews of their German citizenship. Meanwhile the Gestapo (secret police) was set up in April 1933 to monitor possible opponents of the regime, while the Nazis took over the media and the arts.

Hitler also took steps to increase his grip on the Nazi Party. On June 29–30, 1934, the SS rounded up and executed the leaders of the Sturmabteilung and other potential opponents. The so-called Night of the Long Knives shocked Germans. In August, after the death of Hindenburg, Hitler merged the posts of president and chancellor. He took the title of Führer (leader)—and with it absolute power.

→ This civil war poster supports the Falange, Spain's fascist party.

TENSION IN THE PACIFIC

On the other side of the world from Europe, extremism became popular in Japan. Many Japanese believed the country should adopt a form of militaristic nationalism.

Japan had begun modernizing in 1867. Reformers overthrew the old government in the so-called Meiji Restoration. The Japanese also began a program of expansion to gain territory and resources to support their new industrial growth. Japan defeated China in 1895 and Russia in 1905, annexed the Korean peninsula in 1910, and gained German possessions in the Pacific and China during World War I. By 1919, Japanese ambitions had aroused the suspicion of other powers in the region. The United States and Britain were alarmed by Japan's aims in China, particularly after the Twenty-One Demands of 1915, which tried to bring China under Japanese control.

← A Japanese recruit practices firing a machine gun in 1937.

⬆ This print shows the Battle of Tsushima, in which Japan defeated Russia in 1905.

Long-Standing Tensions

There were other causes of tension between Japan and the United States. The Japanese felt their support for the Allies in World War I was not rewarded in the peace treaties. They also felt humiliated by the Washington Naval Treaty of 1922, which restricted the size of the Japanese Navy. Finally, U.S. curbs on Japanese immigration culminated in the 1924 Immigration Act, which halted all Japanese immigration to the United States. A growing Japanese sense of humiliation led to a spread of militaristic values. Japanese conservatives thought

THE TWENTY-ONE DEMANDS

In January 1915, Japan sent China an ultimatum named the Twenty-One Demands. It threatened China with war if China did not give Japan effective control over parts of its territory. The Chinese reluctantly agreed. Although the peace treaties of 1919 removed Japan's newly acquired territory, the episode revealed Japan's ambitions to dominate China.

the country should turn back to traditional values best summed up by Japan's historic knights, the samurai.

Search for Resources

Japan's population had nearly doubled in the 50 years before 1920. Most natural resources had to be imported. For Japan's militarists, such dependency was another blow to national pride. They argued for aggressive expansion to acquire raw materials. They targeted Manchuria in northern China, where Japan already controlled the South Manchuria Railroad.

In 1931, the Imperial Army invaded Manchuria without authorization from the Japanese government and occupied the territory. At home, meanwhile, militarists won more political power. In 1932 Japan rejected the Washington Naval Treaty. In 1933, Japan withdrew from the League of Nations, and in 1937 it began building the world's largest battleships, the *Musashi* and *Yamato*.

China Under attack

Japan launched a massive program of rearmament in the mid-1930s, which increased its need for natural resources. Military planners sought them in China. The Second Sino-Japanese War began in

July 1937. The Japanese rapidly occupied most of China's coastal territories and its main cities, including Beijing and Shanghai. In Nanking, Japanese troops massacred more than 200,000 civilians.

Antagonizing the West

In December 1937, Japanese aircraft sank the gunboat USS *Panay* on the Chang (Yangtze) River in China. The Japanese apologized, but the U.S. government sent funds to the Chinese forces and increased its own naval power in the Pacific.

➡ A convoy of trucks delivers supplies to the Japanese in Manchuria in 1931.

← Japanese students undergo military training in the 1930s. Many school teachers were army veterans.

On September 27, 1940, Japan signed the Tripartite Pact with Germany and Italy. The three countries promised to help each other if the Soviet Union or the United States attacked any one of them. The Japanese also unveiled a plan to create a "Greater East Asia Co-Prosperity Sphere." The plan called for East Asia to rid itself of colonial influences. In reality, it was little more than a Japanese plan to control the whole of East Asia and the Pacific—and all of the region's resources.

THE RAPE OF NANKING

In December 1937, during the war with China, the Japanese drove Chinese troops from the Chinese capital, Nanking. They then began almost two months of violence against the citizens. They killed more than 200,000 people, burying some alive or holding competitions in which soldiers saw who could cut the heads off the most victims.

KEY EVENTS

> **"**I watched the execution of 200 men. The men were lined against a wall and shot. Then a number of Japanese, armed with pistols, trod around the crumpled bodies, pumping bullets into any that were still kicking. A large group of spectators apparently greatly enjoyed the spectacle.**"**
>
> F. Tillman
> New York Times reporter,
> Nanking, December 1937

In reaction to Japan's moves, in July 1940 the U.S. Congress had begun a program of warship production. Japanese analysts calculated that, by 1944, the U.S. Navy would be more than three times the size of Japan's navy. For Japan to achieve military dominance of the Pacific, it would have to act fast.

In April 1941, Japan signed a treaty of nonaggression with the Soviet Union. No longer needing the army to defend

→ By 1941, most of the highest-ranking members of the Japanese cabinet had decided war was inevitable.

it from the Soviets, in July Japan invaded Indochina. The United States increased its financial aid to China. Then, with Britain and the Dutch, it ended imports to Japan. The restrictions were catastrophic for Japan. The United States and the Dutch East Indies provided Japan with 80 percent of its oil.

Toward War

Japan's military planners saw only two options. They could accept the embargo, but would run out of oil by the end of

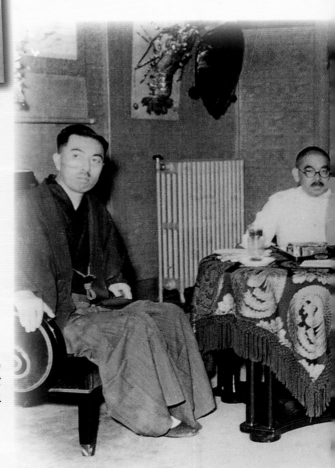

➜ The *Yamato*, which was built in 1937, was the largest battleship in the world at the time.

1942. Or they could go to war to seize territory and resources in the Pacific and Indian Oceans. They chose the option that seemed to be the only hope of success for them: war.

Japan could not hope to defeat the United States in a long war, in which industrial power would prove decisive. Japan's best chance lay in a rapid victory.

After diplomatic talks broke down, U.S. demands that the Japanese withdraw from China and Indochina and break their links with Germany were irrelevant. The Japanese war fleet was already at sea. Its destination was the U.S. Pacific Fleet base at Pearl Harbor in Hawaii.

HITLER'S EXPANSIONISM

Once Hitler came to power in Germany, he began a program of territorial expansion. Europe's other powers, particularly Britain and France, were not sure how to stop him.

Adolf Hitler made no secret of his hatred of the Treaty of Versailles, which limited Germany's armed forces, and his intention to pursue an expansionist foreign policy. In February 1933, Hitler told his generals he planned to take back the Sudetenland—part of Czechoslovakia—and make a union with Austria, before defeating France, Poland, and Russia. Few of his listeners took him seriously. Within a few years, it was clear they were mistaken to have ignored him.

International Relations

In October 1933, Hitler took Germany out of the League of Nations, the body set up to solve international disputes.

→ British prime minister Neville Chamberlain (front, third from left) arrives for talks with Hitler (left) in Munich in 1938.

← Hitler inspects a new warship in 1936. He ignored limits on the size of the German navy.

OCCUPATION OF THE RHINELAND

The Treaty of Versailles created a demilitarized zone in the Rhineland to protect France and the Low Countries. This German territory east and west of the Rhine River was occupied by Allied troops until 1930. On March 7, 1936, Hitler sent 22,000 troops into the Rhineland. France and Britain failed to react, convincing Hitler that he could act as he wished in Europe.

He also sought to make alliances within Europe. The most obvious ally was Italy, governed by Benito Mussolini. There were parallels between Mussolini's fascism and Hitler's Nazism, and the Italians also resented the Versailles treaty. Mussolini also rejected the League of Nations. When he invaded Abyssinia (Ethiopia) in October 1935, he ignored the League's protests.

The alliance between Hitler and Mussolini started badly, however. Mussolini was suspicious of Hitler's plan to create a

Greater Germany through an Anschluss, or union, with Austria. Mussolini saw Austria as a useful buffer between Italy and Germany. When Austrian Nazis murdered the Austrian chancellor, Engelbert Dollfuss, in July 1934, Mussolini mobilized his army on the Austrian border, ready to resist Nazi aggression.

The Saarland

In January 1935, the people of the Saarland, a southwestern region that had been removed from Germany by the Versailles treaty, voted to rejoin Germany. The result was celebrated as a victory for German nationalism. In March, Hitler announced that Germany would no longer accept the military limitations of

↑ Austrian Nazis in the town of Graz celebrate the Anschluss in March 1938.

Versailles. In fact rearmament had been going on for two years. Hitler had calculated that he could disregard Versailles without provoking the European powers into action. He was correct. Italy, France, and Britain were too suspicious of each other's motives to act together against Hitler.

The Rhineland

With his opposition divided, Hitler made his next move. To protect France and the Low Countries (Belgium, the Netherlands, and Luxembourg), the Versailles Treaty had created a demilitarized zone in the Rhineland, German territory along the Rhine River. On March 7, 1936, Hitler sent 22,000 troops into the Rhineland. The move was a gamble. Hitler promised his generals that he would withdraw if there was any opposition. The French did nothing, however, partly because they had no support from Britain.

Hitler and Mussolini

The failure of the democracies to prevent remilitarization of the Rhineland was a strategic victory for Hitler and Europe's dictatorships. In July 1936, Mussolini

⬇ The Nazis began to expand and update the German armed forces, the Wehrmacht.

acknowledged Hitler's claim on Austria. In October, Mussolini and Hitler formed the Rome–Berlin Axis. In November, Germany and Japan signed an Anti-Comintern Pact directed against the Soviet Union. Meanwhile Germany and Italy both supported Francisco Franco's Nationalists in the civil war that began in Spain in July 1936. The war lasted three years before the Nationalists defeated the left-wing Republicans in March 1939.

The Anschluss

The Rome–Berlin Axis opened the way for Hitler's next step after the Rhineland: the Anschluss. In February 1938, Hitler presented the Austrian president with an ultimatum: include Nazi ministers in the government, or Germany would

→ The Munich talks on Czechoslovakia (left to right): Mussolini, Hitler, translator, Chamberlain.

invade. With no backing for Austria from the democracies in Britain and France, the Austrian Nazis went on to take control of the government. They then invited German troops into Austria. On March 13, 1938, Hitler declared Austria a province of the German Reich, or empire. About a month later 99.7 percent of Austrians voted in favor of the Anschluss.

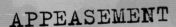

APPEASEMENT

Appeasement is the name given to the policy adopted by Britain, and to an extent by France, toward Hitler's demands. The British believed the Versailles Treaty was harsh toward Germany. They thought that if they gave in to some of Hitler's demands, he would be satisfied. Instead, Hitler saw appeasement as a sign of great weakness in his opponents. He followed each demand with another.

KEY THEMES

Czechoslovakia

The French and British had again failed to stop Hitler. This lack of resistance encouraged Hitler to further expansion. This time his target was the Sudetenland, an area of Czechoslovakia with a large population of Germans. Hitler used the Sudeten Germans as an excuse to claim the whole of Czechoslovakia.

In April 1938, Nazis in the Sudetenland began to demand more control for the Sudeten Germans. The alarmed Czech government of Eduard Benes positioned troops along the German border. Hitler told his generals to prepare for invasion.

Again Britain and France chose not to resist Hitler's demands. As they convinced Benes to make concessions, however, so

Hitler increased his demands. On September 12, Hitler demanded self-determination for the Sudeten Germans and massed his troops on the Czech border.

Fearing imminent war, the British called a conference in Munich on September 30, 1938, to discuss the crisis. The talks were attended by Britain, France, Italy, and Germany. The Czechs were not invited. Hitler got his way: The Czechs were told to evacuate the Sudetenland by October 10 or face war.

After Munich

The Munich agreement marked the beginning of the end of Czech independence. With Hitler's support, Hungary seized territory in the south of Czechoslovakia. On March 15, 1939, Germany occupied the rest of the country. That same month Hitler forced Lithuania to hand the city of Memel—once part of the German state of Prussia—to Germany.

As war appeared increasingly inevitable, France and Britain made overtures to Germany and Italy to

→ Enthusiastic Sudeten Germans welcome German troops to Friedland on October 3, 1938.

NEVILLE CHAMBERLAIN

The man who led Britain into the war was Neville Chamberlain, who became prime minister in 1937. He followed a policy of appeasement and has been widely criticized for underestimating Hitler's territorial ambitions. After appeasement failed he saw war as inevitable, and reluctantly took Britain into the conflict.

1938 he proposed passing Danzig back to Germany. The Poles signed a pact with the Soviet Union and made warlike noises about fighting any loss of territory. France and Britain also finally accepted the need to resist Nazi aggression and committed themselves to save Polish independence.

Approaches to Stalin

Hitler wanted to avoid facing a possible alliance of the Soviet Union, Britain, and France. In August 1939 he offered Stalin

⬇ Nazi banners decorate a street in Danzig. Many Germans in Danzig supported Hitler's claim to the city.

buy time to rearm and to halt expansion, but such moves achieved little. In April 1939, Mussolini put his own territorial expansion into practice, easily overrunning the Balkan state of Albania.

The Question of Poland

Modern Poland had been created by the peace treaties of 1919, and included two areas that were home to about a million Germans: the Baltic port of Danzig (Gdansk in Polish) and the Polish Corridor, a narrow stretch of land linking Poland to Danzig and the sea, and splitting Germany from its state of East Prussia.

Hitler had signed a Nonaggression Pact with Poland in 1934, but in October

→ Motorized German troops move into Poland at the start of the invasion in September 1939.

a deal: If the Soviets allowed Germany to attack western Poland, they would receive eastern Poland and the Baltic states (Lithuania, Latvia, and Estonia).

Munich had convinced Stalin that France and Britain would be unreliable allies. In late August 1939, he signed a German–Soviet Nonaggression Pact. Such an agreement between two nations at opposite political extremes—fascism on one side, communism on the other—shocked the world. It also left Hitler with a free hand in Poland. All he needed was an excuse to invade before Poland and its allies could make defensive preparations.

THE GERMAN BLITZKRIEG

From September 1939 to May 1940, Germany's land and air forces won a series of rapid victories that left them in control of much of Europe.

On September 1, 1939, German troops staged a fake raid on a German radio station near the Polish border that was then blamed on Poles. The raid was the excuse for 1.5 million German soldiers to invade Poland. The Luftwaffe (German air force) took control of the skies within a few days. panzer (tank) divisions pushed through enemy lines, aiming for key bridges over Poland's rivers. In the confusion, hundreds of thousands of refugees clogged up roads, making it difficult for the Polish to build up organized resistance.

The Poles were outnumbered and largely abandoned by their British and French allies. Although they could do little to

➔ A horse-drawn German supply column crosses a river in Poland.

↓ German Panzer I and II tanks advance in Poland in September 1939.

help Poland, Britain and France declared war on Germany on September 3. By the second week of September, the city of Warsaw was surrounded by German forces advancing from the north, west, and south. German bombers pounded the city day and night.

THE SOVIETS INVADE

On September 17, the Soviet dictator Joseph Stalin, sent his Red Army into eastern Poland. Germany and the Soviet Union had secretly agreed to divide up Poland between them in the German–Soviet Nonaggression Pact. Polish resistance collapsed. In the last week

EYEWITNESS ACCOUNT

"We were terrified. German planes kept firing down at us with their machine guns, and they seemed to shriek like wild animals as they dived with their bombs and bullets. We decided to run home, and we made our way through streets filled with panick-stricken people who were shrieking hysterically."

Kalmen Wewryk
Chelm,
Poland, 1939

of September Warsaw surrendered. The Germans and Soviets divided up Poland. As far as Hitler and Stalin were concerned, Poland no longer existed.

War in the West

There followed a seven-month lull as the Germans prepared for a campaign in the west. The period was nicknamed the "Phoney War." German strategy was similar to their strategy at the start of World War I in 1914: They would attack west from Germany into Belgium, then swing south into northern France. They

⬇ German forces march into the Polish capital, Warsaw, after the fall of the city.

extended the plan to include an invasion of neutral Holland and an armored thrust through the Ardennes to the south that would destroy the Allied position.

By May 1940, the two sides—each with about 3 million men—faced each other along the border from the North Sea to Switzerland. Hitler's western offensive began at dawn on May 10, 1940. The Luftwaffe attacked Belgian and Dutch airfields, and paratroopers seized key bridges and airfields. Soon the Belgian Army fell back, to be reinforced by the British Expeditionary Force (BEF) and the French First Army. After just four days, the Dutch army surrendered. The Dutch government and navy fled to England.

The German advance had drawn the BEF and French troops into Belgium. The Germans sprang their trap. On May 10, three panzer corps advanced through the Ardennes to the Meuse River on the border. On May 13, the infantry began to cross the river. By May 15, six panzer divisions were moving west into France, behind the Allied defenders.

⬆ The Junkers Ju-87 Stuka dive-bomber was a key part of Germany's Blitzkrieg tactics.

Race to the Channel

The Allies were thrown into chaos. Allied troops were ordered to counterattack against the German breakthrough. On May 21, British tanks struck toward Arras

BLITZKRIEG TACTICS

The advance into Poland was Germany's first use of Blitzkrieg, or "lightning war." This new approach to warfare depended on breaking through enemy lines and penetrating quickly into enemy territory. It was based on the speed of German tanks, supported by dive-bombers and motorized infantry. The quick-moving advance simply left pockets of resistance to be dealt with by the main infantry as it raced ahead. The tactics were highly successful, and allowed the German armies to rapidly overrun Poland, the Low Countries, and France.

KEY THEMES

DUNKIRK

The withdrawal to Dunkirk was a traumatic experience for the Allied troops. By the end of May they were being shelled and bombed in a small bridgehead. However, Hitler's order to halt his panzers outside Dunkirk gave most of the trapped Allied troops a chance to escape. A fleet of civilian ships helped the Royal Navy rescue more than 220,000 British and 113,000 French troops.

was evacuated. With his country all but overrun, the Belgian king surrendered on May 28.

Fall of France

The Germans turned their attention south toward France. An advance began on June 5. French defense reached the breaking point and the government ordered a retreat. By June 14, German troops were marching past the Arc de Triomphe in Paris. On June 16, the government resigned. Marshal Philippe Pétain became president and negotiated an armistice, which was signed on

but ran into a concentration of German tanks. The attack shocked Hitler, who ordered the advance to halt. The German High Command instead ordered the army to focus on the Allied troops in northern France. French morale was on the verge of complete collapse.

The British government was equally confused. The new prime minister, Winston Churchill, ordered the BEF to fall back to Dunkirk on the coast, where it

→ These vehicles were abandoned on the beach at Dunkirk by retreating British troops.

← German troops parade past the Arc de Triomphe in Paris in June 1940.

June 22. France was split in two. The north and west, including Paris, were placed under German occupation, while the southeast was governed by Pétain from the town of Vichy. Pétain's government was largely influenced by Germany, however.

In just two months German armies had conquered much of northern Europe. For the time being Hitler was the master of much of the continent.

EYEWITNESS ACCOUNT

"We did not go through the big cities with our horses and artillery, but stayed in the countryside. The farms had been abandoned, and we often encountered the refugees from them. They had left their homes because they heard the sound of battle coming toward them. It was sad to see them."

Siegfried Knappe
German soldier in France,
May 1940

FINLAND AND SCANDINAVIA

Germany's planned conquest of northern Europe called for the rapid overthrow of Finland and other Scandinavian countries, particularly Norway.

After the German and Soviet occupation of Poland, Stalin took advantage of the free hand Hitler had given him in Eastern Europe. He demanded that Finland allow Soviet troops to occupy naval bases and a key border region. The Finns refused and quickly mobilized their small forces.

On October 30, 1939, Soviet troops surged across the border. Finnish ski troops mounted hit and run attacks on Soviet troops as they moved through the forested landscape. In a month of fighting, 27,500 Red Army troops were killed. They had been poorly trained and were badly equipped.

→ Finnish ski-troops use reindeer as pack animals during the campaign against the Soviet invaders.

A new Soviet offensive began on February 1, 1940. This time they used large-scale artillery barrages to destroy enemy strongpoints before launching a mass attack. The Finns were worn down. They reluctantly signed a nonaggression pact with Stalin on March 12.

Preparations for War

Over the winter of 1939 and into 1940, the British and French began to switch their factories to the production of weapons and ammunition. Although little happened during the period known as the Phoney War, in October 1939 the

⬇ German troops take cover beside a wall during fighting in Norway.

German submarine *U-47* made a raid into the British anchorage at Scapa Flow in the Orkney Islands, in the north of Scotland. *U-47* torpedoed and sank the Royal Navy battleship, HMS *Royal Oak*.

Focus on Norway

The Soviet attack on Finland now forced the Germans and Allies to focus on Scandinavia. There was great sympathy for the Finns in Britain and France, and leaders in London and Paris also wanted to intervene in Scandinavia to damage Germany's war industry. Germany imported regular iron-ore shipments from neutral Sweden. In winter the ore had to pass through the Norwegian port of Narvik. Hitler saw the supply of iron as a strategic priority. Convinced the Allies

VIDKUN QUISLING

Vidkun Quisling was the leader of the tiny Norwegian fascist party. When the Germans invaded, Quisling declared himself prime minister. In 1942 the Germans allowed his party to become Norway's only legal political organization. He imposed strict measures to crush resistance to Nazi rule in Norway. Hated by fellow Norwegians, Quisling gave his name to a general term meaning "traitor."

were about to close Norwegian ports to German shipping, Hitler ordered his generals to strike north into Norway.

The German invasion of Norway began on the early morning of April 9. The German plan relied on surprise to avoid the British Royal Navy and to prevent Norwegian forces from mobilizing. The sudden appearance of naval task forces took Norwegian defenders by surprise and allowed airfields to be captured by the Germans intact. At the same time German troops occupied airbases and ports in Denmark. Denmark was overrun within 24 hours. Soon the Luftwaffe had taken control of the skies over southern and central Norway.

→ The German battleship *Bismarck* was completed in June 1940. It was the largest warship ever built in Germany.

Allied Response

The German Navy suffered severe losses to British warships in the Norwegian waters. But despite this setback, much of southern Norway was under German control by April 16, 1940. The first British and French troops arrived on April 15 in central Norway but on April 30 German forces at Trondheim advanced and linked up with forces in Oslo. Norwegian forces in central and southern Norway began to surrender. By mid-May, the British and French had deployed about 25,000 men to Narvik. The port fell to the Allies on May 27–28, but this victory was not to last long.

Allied Withdrawal

On May 10, Germany had invaded France and the Low Countries. Every British and French soldier was needed to fight the Germans in France. The Allies pulled out of Norway. By June 8, the Norwegian government had agreed a ceasefire with Germany. The last Allied troops left on June 8, but the evacuation fleet was surprised by the German battle cruisers *Scharnhorst* and *Gneisenau*. The British aircraft carrier HMS *Glorious* and two destroyers were sunk with the loss of 1,515 lives.

The Norwegian campaign had been a disaster for the Allies, who had been disorganized and ill equipped.

⬆ Winston Churchill (left) became prime minister of Britain in May 1940.

A significant result of the campaign was the fall of the British government and its prime minister, Neville Chamberlain. A new leader was selected to form a government of national unity supported by all political parties. The new prime minister was Winston Churchill, who immediately began planning to resist a German advance in North Africa. He would become Hitler's chief adversary.

TIMELINE OF WORLD WAR II

1939 **September:** German troops invade and overrun Poland; Britain and France declare war on Germany; the Soviet Union invades eastern Poland. The Battle of the Atlantic begins.

April: Germany invades Denmark and Norway; Allied troops land in Norway.

May: Germany invades Luxembourg, the Netherlands, Belgium, and France; Allied troops are evacuated at Dunkirk.

June: Allied troops leave Norway; Italy enters the war; France signs an armistice with Germany; Italy bombs Malta in the Mediterranean.

July: German U-boats (submarines) inflict heavy losses on Allied convoys in the Atlantic; The Battle of Britain begins.

September: Luftwaffe air raids begin the Blitz—the bombing of British cities; Italian troops advance from Libya into Egypt.

October: Italy invades Greece.

December: British troops defeat the Italians at Sidi Barrani, Egypt.

1941 **January:** Allied units capture Tobruk in Libya.

February: Rommel's Afrika Korps arrive in Tripoli.

March: The Afrika Korps drive British troops back from El Agheila.

April: Axis units invade Yugoslavia; German forces invade Greece; the Afrika Korps besiege Tobruk.

June: German troops invade the Soviet Union.

September: Germans besiege Leningrad and attack Moscow.

December: Japanese aircraft attack the U.S. Pacific Fleet at Pearl Harbor; Japanese forces invade the Philippines, Malaya, and Thailand, and defeat the British garrison in Hong Kong.

1942 **January:** Japan invades Burma; Rommel launches a new offensive in Libya; Allied troops leave Malaya.

February: Singapore surrenders to the Japanese.

April: The Bataan Peninsula in the Philippines falls to the Japanese.

May: U.S. and Japanese fleets clash at the Battle of the Coral Sea.

June: The U.S. Navy defeats the Japanese at the Battle of Midway; Rommel recaptures Tobruk.

September–October: Allied forces defeat Axis troops at El Alamein, Egypt, the first major Allied victory of the war.

November: U.S. and British troops land in Morocco and Algeria.

1943

February: The German Sixth Army surrenders at Stalingrad; the Japanese leave Guadalcanal in the Solomon Islands.

May: Axis forces in Tunisia surrender.

July: The Red Army wins the Battle of Kursk; Allied troops land on the Italian island of Sicily.

August: German forces occupy Italy; the Soviets retake Kharkov.

September: Allied units begin landings on mainland Italy; Italy surrenders, prompting a German invasion of northern Italy.

November: U.S. carrier aircraft attack the port of Rabaul in the Solomon Islands.

1944

January: The German siege of Leningrad ends.

February: U.S. forces conquer the Marshall Islands.

March: The Soviet offensive reaches the Dniester River; Allied aircraft bomb the monastery at Monte Cassino in Italy.

June: U.S. troops enter the city of Rome; D-Day–the Allied invasion of northern Europe; U.S. aircraft defeat the Japanese fleet at the Battle of the Philippine Sea.

July: Soviet tanks enter Poland.

August: Japanese troops retreat in Burma; Allied units liberate towns in France, Belgium, and the Netherlands.

October: The Japanese suffer defeat at the Battle of Leyte Gulf.

December: German troops counterattack in the Ardennes.

1945

January: The U.S. Army lands on Luzon in the Philippines; most of Poland and Czechoslovakia are liberated by the Allies.

February: U.S. troops land on Iwo Jima; Soviet troops strike west across Germany; the U.S. Army heads toward the Rhine River.

April: U.S. troops land on the island of Okinawa; Mussolini is shot by partisans; Soviet troops assault Berlin; Hitler commits suicide.

May: All active German forces surrender.

June: Japanese resistance ends in Burma and on Okinawa.

August: Atomic bombs are dropped on Hiroshima and Nagasaki; Japan surrenders.

GLOSSARY

advance A general move forward by a military force.

Allies One of the two groups of combatants in the war. The main Allies were Britain, the Soviet Union, the United States, British Empire troops, and free forces from occupied nations.

annexed Seized territory to add to one's own.

armistice A halt in fighting agreed to by both sides in a war.

armor A term referring to armored vehicles, such as tanks.

army group Two or more armies grouped together.

artillery Large weapons such as big guns and howitzers.

Axis One of the two groups of combatants in the war. The leading Axis powers were Germany, Italy, and Japan.

blitzkrieg A German word meaning "lightning war." It referred to the tactic of rapid land advance supported by great airpower.

concentration camps Places in which large numbers of people are imprisoned in a small space.

empire A group of a number of countries governed by a single country.

coup The sudden and violent seizure of power from a government.

empire A group of a number of countries governed by a single country.

evacuation Moving someone from danger to a safe position.

independence The state of self-government for a people or nation.

infantry Soldiers who are trained to fight on foot or in vehicles.

mandate An authorization to perform to govern a territory; a mandated territory.

militarism A political belief that military concerns should shape society, which should be organized with strict rules and discipline.

motorization The introduction of motor vehicles.

occupation The seizure and control of an area by military force.

offensive A planned military attack.

overtures Initial moves that are preparations for something more substantial.

partisans Irregular fighters who carry out armed resistance against an occupying force.

reparations Payment made for war damage by a defeated state.

resources Natural materials that are the basis of economic wealth, such as oil, rubber, and agricultural produce.

strategy A detailed plan for achieving success.

ultimatum A demand which, if it is not met, will lead to war.

FURTHER RESOURCES

Books

Adams, Simon. *Causes, Course, and Consequences* (World War II). Sea to Sea Publications, 2009.

Countdown to Catastrophe (World War II). Marshall Cavendish Corporation, 2010.

George, Enzo. *World War II in Europe and North Africa: Preserving Democracy* (Voices of War). Cavendish Square Publishing, 2014.

Hynson, Colin. *World War II: A Primary Source History* (In Their Own Words). Gareth Stevens Publishing, 2005.

Price, Sean. *Adolf Hitler* (Wicked History). Franklin Watts, 2010.

Rice, Earle. *Blitzkrieg! Hitler's Lightning War* (Monumental Milestones). Mitchell Lane Publishers, 2007.

Websites

www.ducksters.com/history/ world_war_ii/
Ducksters.com links to articles about the war.

www.historyonthenet.com/ ww2/home_front.htm
History.com page of links about aspects of World War II.

www.socialstudiesforkids.com/ subjects/worldwarii.htm/
Index of articles about U.S. involvement in the conflict.

http://www.pbs.org/thewar/
PBS pages on the war to support the Ken Burns' film, *The War.*

http://www.pbs.org/wgbh/ amex/dday/timeline/
Timeline of the war on PBS pages from The American Experience.

INDEX